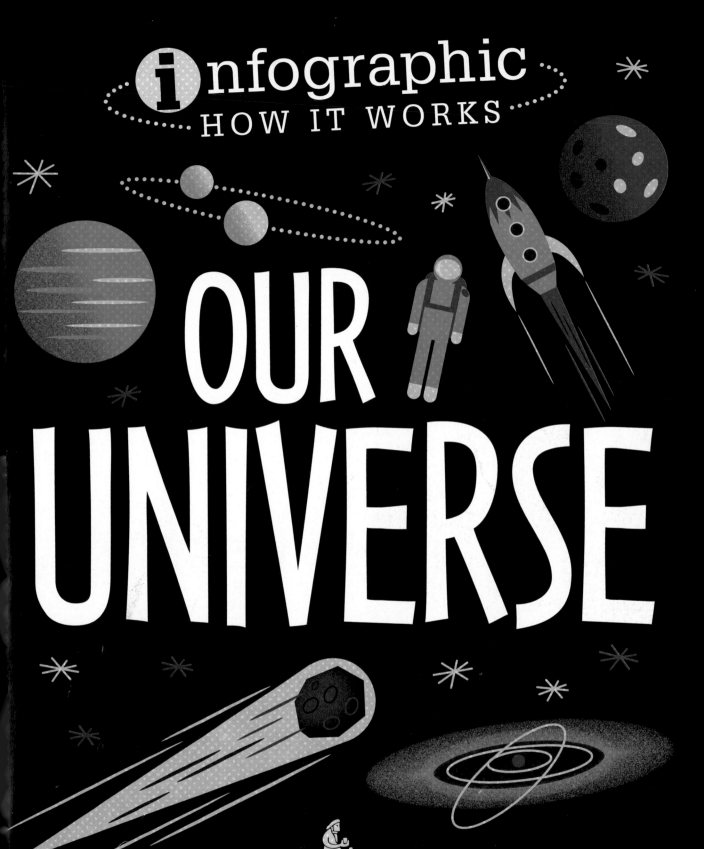

infographic
HOW IT WORKS

OUR UNIVERSE

WAYLAND

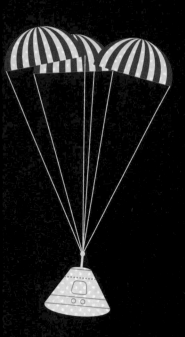

First published in Great Britain
in 2016 by Wayland
Copyright © Wayland, 2016
All rights reserved

Editor: Liza Miller
Produced by Tall Tree Ltd
Editor: Jon Richards
Designer: Ed Simkins

ISBN: 978 0 7502 9882 7
10 9 8 7 6 5 4 3 2 1

Wayland
An imprint of Hachette
Children's Group
Part of Hodder and Stoughton
Carmelite House
50 Victoria Embankment
London EC4Y 0DZ

An Hachette UK Company
www.hachette.co.uk
www.hachettechildrens.co.uk

Printed and bound in China

CONTENTS

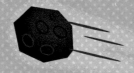

SPACE IS BIG!

Strap yourself in for a trip across the universe, as this book shows you how planets, stars and galaxies work, and how we've been able to study and explore objects throughout the cosmos.

LIGHT-YEAR

Space is so enormous that scientists don't know exactly how big – or even what shape – it is. To measure the vast distances in space, normal units, such as kilometres, aren't very helpful. Instead, we use the light-year, which is the distance that light travels in one year.

Light travels about 300,000 km in a second, which means that one light-year is about nine trillion km.

Sun

Earth

Light from the Sun takes 8.5 minutes to reach us.

FAMILY OF OBJECTS

Space is largely empty because it is so massive, but there are still lots of different objects inside it. They range from tiny asteroids and comets measuring only a few metres across to enormous galaxies that are millions of light-years in size.

moon

planet

**radio
telescope**

**Hubble
Space
Telescope**

telescope

STUDYING SPACE

Scientists who study space are called astronomers. They use a whole host of instruments and equipment to view space, including telescopes and satellites in orbit around Earth. We have sent probes to explore the other planets in the solar system, land on some of them, and even drive over their surfaces.

The space probe *Voyager 1* is the most distant man-made object. Launched in 1977, it is now about 19 billion km from Earth. That sounds like a lot, but *Voyager 1* won't reach another star for 40,000 years!

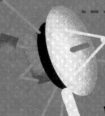

Voyager 1

star

galaxy

HOW TO LOOK INTO SPACE

Optical telescopes allow us to see distant objects using visible light. Telescopes also magnify things because they collect more light than the human eye. The larger the lens or mirror, the greater the magnification.

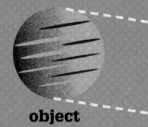

light rays

object

lens

aperture

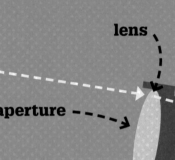

1 LIGHT RAYS

Rays of light from space enter a refracting telescope through the opening at the front called the aperture.

2 LENS

A specially shaped piece of glass, called a lens, sits at the front of the telescope. It bends, or refracts, rays of light so that they travel down the telescope's tube.

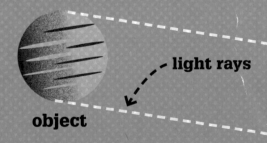

light rays

object

The Gran Telescopio Canarias is the largest optical telescope in the world. Its aperture measures 10.4 m across — that's bigger than a bus!

TRY THIS ...

❸ EYEPIECE

Telescopes that use lenses to collect light are called refracting telescopes. A lens in the eyepiece adjusts light rays so that they form a clear picture.

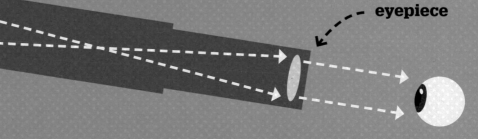

refracting telescope

eyepiece

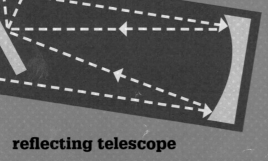

eyepiece

mirror

reflecting telescope

❶ MIRROR

In a reflecting telescope, a large curved mirror at the back of the telescope reflects light rays up to a secondary mirror.

❷ IMAGE

Another mirror reflects light rays towards a lens inside the eyepiece. This focuses them so that they produce a clear image.

7

HOW SPACE ROCKETS WORK

Getting into space takes a huge amount of energy. Rockets blast their way through the atmosphere carrying satellites, probes and astronauts into orbit around Earth — and out into space.

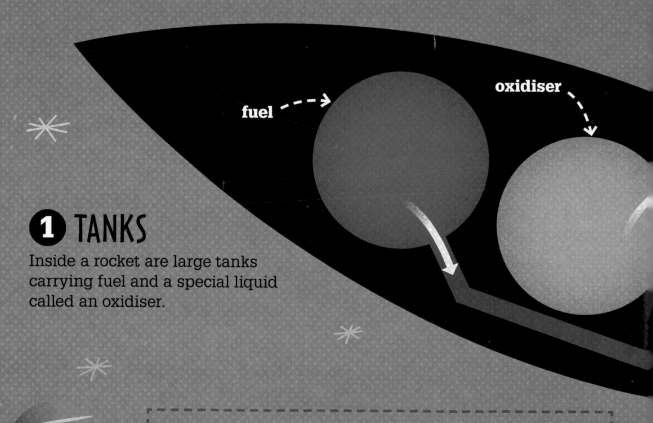

fuel

oxidiser

❶ TANKS

Inside a rocket are large tanks carrying fuel and a special liquid called an oxidiser.

The massive *Saturn V* rockets were more than 110 m tall. They were built to blast astronauts to the Moon and to launch the *Skylab* space station into orbit.

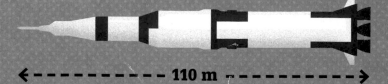

← - - - - - - - - — 110 m - - - - - - - - →

Push against a wall and feel yourself being pushed backwards. This is the principle that pushes rockets through the air: for every action there is an equal and opposite reaction.

② PUMP

The fuel and oxidiser are pumped through pipes into a part called the combustion chamber.

③ MIXED

The fuel and oxidiser are mixed together in the combustion chamber and set alight.

⑤ THRUST

As the gas roars out of the nozzle, it pushes the rocket forwards and into space.

pump

combustion chamber

hot gas

nozzle

④ BURNING

The burning mixture produces a blast of hot gas, which roars out of the nozzle at the back of the rocket.

HOW TO GET INTO ORBIT

A rocket needs to hit a speed of 28,000 km/h to get into orbit. It uses several 'stages' to help it reach this speed. Each stage has its own engines and fuel.

② BOOSTER

Two minutes after launch, the first stage booster rockets run out of fuel. They separate and fall back down to Earth, landing safely in the ocean.

① BLAST OFF

The rocket blasts off vertically. As it gains height, it starts to lean over and it turns towards the direction of its final orbit.

2nd stage

booster

1st stage

launch site

The International Space Station is in low Earth orbit, 400 km up.

Earth

GPS satellites are in medium Earth orbit, 20,000 km up.

At high Earth orbit, 36,000 km up, are satellites that remain above one spot on Earth as they orbit. Satellites here are used to pass on communications signals and monitor the weather.

3rd stage

❸ INTO ORBIT

As the rocket nears its final height, the second stage runs out of fuel and separates, leaving the third stage to enter orbit. This final stage is much smaller than the first and second stages.

TRY THIS ...

HOW TO LAND ON A PLANET

After travelling millions of kilometres to reach a distant moon or planet, spacecraft need to land carefully so that their equipment isn't damaged and their work can be carried out.

1 PARACHUTES

If the moon or planet has an atmosphere, a spacecraft can use a parachute to slow its fall. Many spacecraft returning to Earth use parachutes so that they land safely.

parachutes

2 ROCKETS

Some probes use retro-rockets to slow them down. As the spacecraft falls, the downward-pointing rockets fire, slowing the descent so that the craft lands safely.

retro-rockets

Make your own parachute by using string to tie the corners of a paper towel to a small toy. Throw the toy in the air and see how the parachute slows its fall.

③ AIRBAGS

When it landed on Mars in 1997, *Mars Pathfinder* used a parachute and rockets to slow its fall. Then, when it was about 350 m above the ground, it inflated a number of airbags. These protected the robot probe as it bounced to a safe landing.

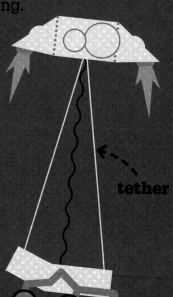

④ TETHER

The *Mars Science Laboratory* used a parachute to slow its fall at first. It then fired several small rocket engines to slow things down even more, before the robot rover it carried was lowered to the surface by a tether.

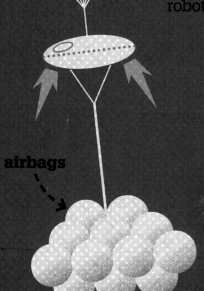

airbags

tether

HOW PLANETS ARE MADE

About 4.5 billion years ago, Earth and all the other planets, asteroids, moons and comets making up the solar system formed around the Sun.

1 GAS AND DUST

Surrounding the early Sun was a large swirling disc of gas and dust.

2 CLUMPS

Over time, clumps started to form in this disc. These clumps, or protoplanets, attracted more and more dust and rock, getting bigger as they did so.

clump

clump

3 PLANETS

The planets that formed closer to the Sun were made from rocky material, while those further out were larger, and contained more gas and icy material.

1. Mercury

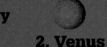

2. Venus

3. Earth

4. Mars

5. Jupiter

6. Saturn

7. Uranus

8. Neptune

The solar system contains eight major planets (shown here in order from the Sun outwards).

Not to scale.

Far out in the solar system is an object called Pluto, which used to be called a planet. In 2006, however, Pluto's status was changed to a dwarf planet.

④ IGNITION

When the Sun ignited and started to shine (see pages 20–21), it blew away much of the excess dust and gas, leaving the planets and other bodies behind.

TRY THIS ...

If the Sun was the size of a basketball, then Jupiter, the largest planet, would be the size of a table-tennis ball. How big do you think Earth would be?

HOW COMETS MAKE TAILS

A comet's tail can stretch for more than 10 million km.

Comets are frozen balls of ice and dust. They usually travel far out in space, but every now and then one is pushed towards the Sun, where it forms a spectacular sight in the night sky.

① SNOWBALLS

As a comet approaches the Sun, heat from the star causes the ice and dust on the comet's surface to boil away into space.

dust
tail

gas
tail

② TAILS

As the gas and dust boils off the comet, they form two long tails that stream behind the comet's head.

Sun

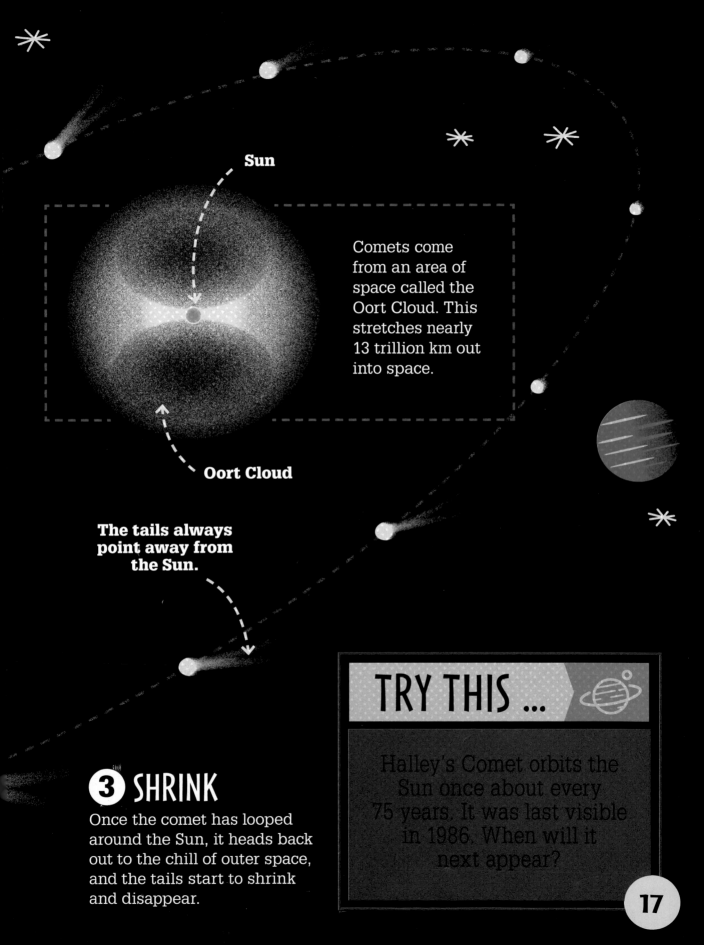

Sun

Comets come from an area of space called the Oort Cloud. This stretches nearly 13 trillion km out into space.

Oort Cloud

The tails always point away from the Sun.

❸ SHRINK

Once the comet has looped around the Sun, it heads back out to the chill of outer space, and the tails start to shrink and disappear.

TRY THIS ...

Halley's Comet orbits the Sun once about every 75 years. It was last visible in 1986. When will it next appear?

HOW A STAR IS BORN

Stars are born inside huge clouds of gas and dust called nebulae. These clouds glow with beautiful colours, because they are lit up by energy from the new stars.

❶ CLUMPS

Inside the clouds are clumps where dust and gas has gathered together.

❷ MASSIVE

The clumps start to attract more and more material, increasing in size over a long period of time.

Orion

Stars in the night sky form patterns called constellations. One of the easiest to spot is Orion. Can you find this in the night sky?

❹ SHINE

When the pressure and temperature get high enough, atoms at the centre of the star fuse together (see pages 20–21). This releases huge amounts of energy, and the new star starts to shine.

❸ HOTTER

As the clumps get bigger, material at the centre of each clump starts to get hotter, and the pressure gets very high.

HOW TO MAKE THE SUN SHINE

The Sun is a huge ball of burning gases. At its centre is a super-hot core, which produces the energy that makes it shine.

1 HOT CORE

In the core, huge pressure squeezes hydrogen atoms until they fuse together to create helium atoms. This fusion also releases enormous amounts of energy in the form of photons.

convective zone

radiative zone

photon

photon

core

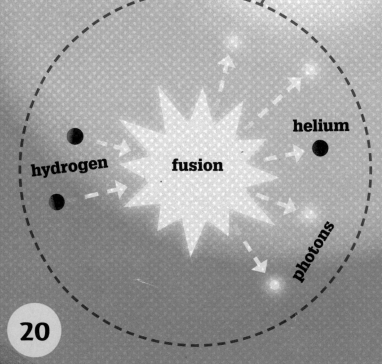

hydrogen

fusion

helium

photons

2 TO THE SURFACE

Photons shoot off in all directions from the core. They crash into each other and can take thousands of years to pass through different zones before reaching the surface.

③ LIGHT AND HEAT

When photons reach the Sun's surface, they fly off into space at the speed of light. When the photons hit Earth, they warm up the planet.

The outer layer of the Sun is called the photosphere.

Earth

The temperature at the surface is about 6,000 °C.

TRY THIS ...

If light travels about 18 million km in a minute, how long does it take to travel from the Sun to the Earth, which is 153 million km away?

HOW A STAR DIES

As long as a star has fuel to burn in its core, it will continue to shine. However, when it runs out of fuel, its core becomes unstable, leading to some big changes. These changes depend on how massive that star is.

1 SWELL

When a star that's as massive as our Sun starts to run out of fuel, it begins to swell to many times its original size.

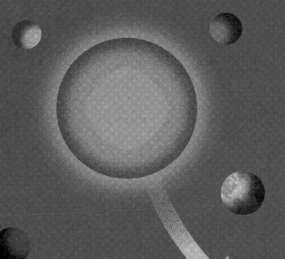

inner planets

The Sun will become a white dwarf in 7 billion years' time. Before then, it will expand massively to engulf the innermost planets, including Earth.

TRY THIS ...

When you next see a fire or a barbecue, watch
how one of the logs or coals cools down once it's
stopped burning. It will glow and stay very hot for
a while, but eventually it will cool down and go
dark – just like a white dwarf star.

4 COOL

White dwarf stars do not create heat by
nuclear fusion. Instead, they cool down
gradually over time, leaving behind a
cold, dark remnant.

2 NEBULA

Eventually, the star throws off
its outer layers, creating a
brightly coloured ring-shaped
cloud called a planetary nebula.

**A white dwarf
star is about the
same size as
Earth.**

**planetary
nebula**

**cold
remnant**

3 DWARF STAR

At the same time, what's
left of the star shrinks
down to leave a tiny
white dwarf star.

HOW A BLACK HOLE IS MADE

Black holes are strange objects that have so much mass that their gravity becomes incredibly strong – they pull everything into them, even light. These strange objects are created by some of the most violent events in the universe: supernovae.

❶ SWELL

Stars that are more massive than our Sun may end their lives very violently. As the star runs out of fuel, it starts to swell, creating a red supergiant star.

② COLLAPSE

After a while, the whole core of the star collapses and then creates a massive explosion, called a supernova. What the supernova leaves behind depends on how massive the original star was.

③ NEUTRON STAR

If the original star was up to three times more massive than our Sun, then it will leave behind a neutron star.

A pulsar is a type of neutron star. It sends out powerful jets of radiation, creating pulsing radio signals as it spins around, like the beams of light from a lighthouse.

A black hole sends out powerful beams of energy.

Light cannot escape a black hole.

④ BLACK HOLE

If the original star was more than three times as massive as our Sun, the supernova will leave behind a black hole.

TRY THIS ...

HOW TO FORM A GALAXY

Galaxies are huge collections of stars that swirl around each other. The biggest galaxies can contain more than a trillion stars.

❶ CLOUDS

In the early part of a spiral galaxy's life, huge clouds of gas, dust and young stars collect together.

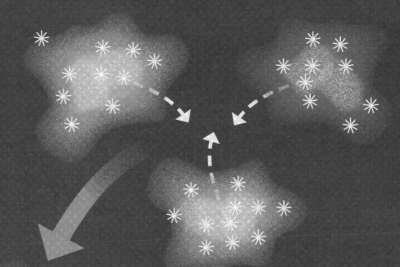

❷ SPIN

The stars and dust start to rotate around a central region.

❸ BULGE

As the huge cloud rotates, it collects together, forming a central bulge that is surrounded by a disc.

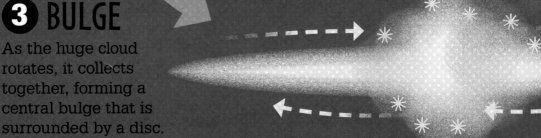

There are three main types of galaxy: spiral galaxies, elliptical galaxies (which are shaped like oval balls) and irregular galaxies (which have no shape at all). About 75 per cent of all galaxies are spiral.

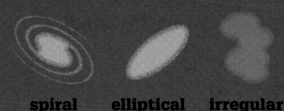

spiral   **elliptical**   **irregular**

Our own galaxy is about 100,000 light-years across. This means it takes light 100,000 years to travel across it.

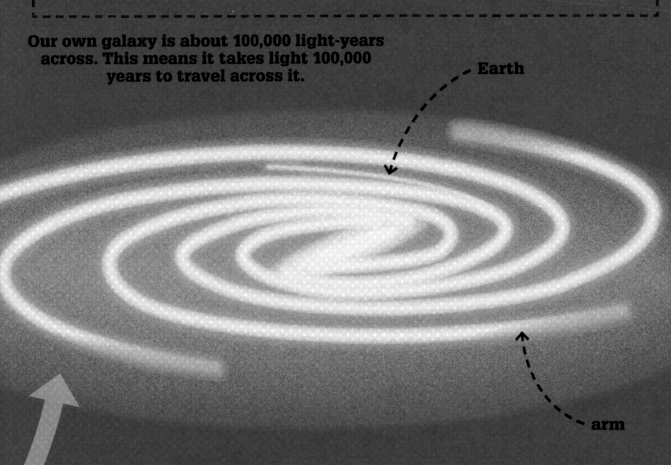

Earth

arm

❹ SPIRAL

As it spins, the stars in the disc collect together to form arms, which spiral out from the central bulge.

TRY THIS ...

HOW THE UNIVERSE EXPLODED

Astronomers believe that the universe was formed in an enormous explosion called the Big Bang. This happened about 13.8 billion years ago, and it formed everything that makes up the universe.

❶ THE START

The universe began with a tiny object called a singularity.

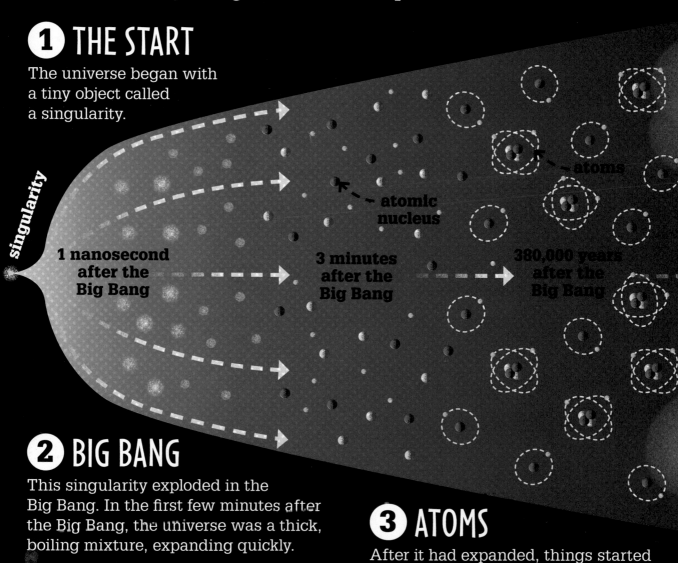

singularity

1 nanosecond after the Big Bang

atomic nucleus

3 minutes after the Big Bang

atoms

380,000 years after the Big Bang

❷ BIG BANG

This singularity exploded in the Big Bang. In the first few minutes after the Big Bang, the universe was a thick, boiling mixture, expanding quickly.

❸ ATOMS

After it had expanded, things started to cool down, and this allowed the first atoms to form.

4 STARS

About 300 million years after the Big Bang, the first stars started to shine.

Astronomers believe that there are at least 100 billion planets in our Milky Way alone. Design your own planet and write about the conditions you might find there.

stars

early galaxies

1 billion years after the Big Bang

300 million years after the Big Bang

5 GALAXIES

Over the next hundred million years, these stars clumped together to form the first galaxies.

GLOSSARY

AIRBAGS
Inflatable bags that protect objects in the event of a collision.

APERTURE
The opening at the front of a telescope.

ASTEROID
A small piece of rock orbiting the Sun.

ASTRONAUT
A person who travels into space.

ASTRONOMERS
Scientists who study space.

BLACK HOLE
A object in space with so much gravity that not even light can escape.

BOOSTER ROCKETS
Rockets strapped to a spacecraft that are used to blast it into orbit.

COMBUSTION CHAMBER
The part of a rocket where the fuel is set alight, creating the blast of hot gases that pushes the rocket forwards.

COMET
A small piece of ice and dust orbiting the Sun. As it approaches the Sun, it produces long tails made up of gas and dust.

CONVECTIVE ZONE
A layer inside a star where the energy swirls around in huge convection currents.

ELECTROMAGNETIC SPECTRUM
The entire range of light energy, such as visible light, which we can see, as well as invisible forms, such as radio waves, gamma rays and microwaves.

FUSION
When atoms are squeezed together until they fuse. This releases huge amounts of energy.

GALAXIES
Very large groups of stars.

GRAVITY
The force which attracts one object to another, depending on how massive they are. The more massive an object, the more gravity it has.

LENS
A specially shaped piece of glass which can bend, or refract, light.

LIGHT-YEAR
The distance that light travels in a year. This unit is used to measure the distances across space.

MAGNIFY
To increase the size of something.

MASS
The amount of matter an object has.

NEBULA
A large cloud of dust and gas (plural: nebulae).

NEUTRON STAR
A type of very dense star, whose atoms are very tightly packed together.

NOZZLE
The part of a rocket which directs the blast of hot gases.

ORBIT
The path of one object around another, such as a planet around a star.

OXIDISER
A chemical that helps another material to catch fire.

PHOTON
A tiny particle which carries light.

PLANETARY NEBULA
A ring-shaped cloud of dust and gas produced in the last stages of some stars' lives.

PROBE
A robot spacecraft.

PROTOPLANET
The name given to a planet at a very early stage in its life.

PULSAR
A type of neutron star which produces energy beams that appear to pulse as the star spins around.

RADIATIVE ZONE
A layer inside a star where the energy is moved around by radiation or conduction.

RETRO-ROCKETS
Rockets that point in the opposite direction to a spacecraft's movement and are designed to slow the spacecraft down.

ROVER
A robotic probe that is designed to drive around the surface of another planet or moon.

SATELLITE
An object that goes around, or orbits, another. Satellites can be natural, such as moons, or they can be artificial, such as weather and communications satellites.

SUPERNOVA
The powerful explosion at the end of a massive star's life (plural: supernovae).

TELESCOPES
Devices used to study objects that are far away. Optical telescopes are used to look at visible objects. Other types of telescope can study invisible forms of light, such as infrared and ultra-violet light.

TETHER
A cord linking two objects.

UNIVERSE
Everything that exists, including planets, stars and galaxies.

WHITE DWARF
The small, dying remains of a star.

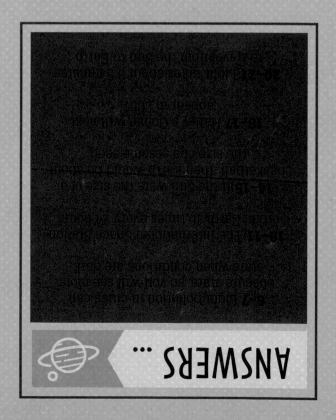

ANSWERS

INDEX

WEBSITES

www.nasa.gov
The website of the National Aeronautics and Space
Administration. It contains the latest information on
space missions and discoveries, from the planets
closest to us to the most distant galaxies.

www.kidsastronomy.com
Packed full of educational games, activities,
worksheets and movies, this website is the perfect
gateway to the wonders of the universe for children.

FOR MORE AMAZING INFOGRAPHICS, TRY THE FACT-PACKED MAPOGRAPHICA SERIES.

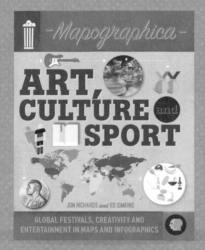

978 0 7502 9148 4

978 0 7502 9145 3

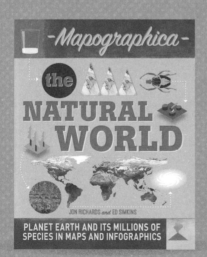

978 0 7502 9154 5

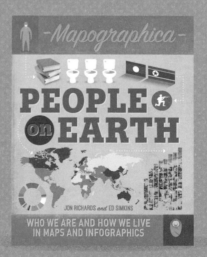

978 0 7502 9151 4

WAYLAND

www.waylandbooks.co.uk